FLYING COLOURS

AIRLINE COLOUR SCHEMES OF THE 1990s

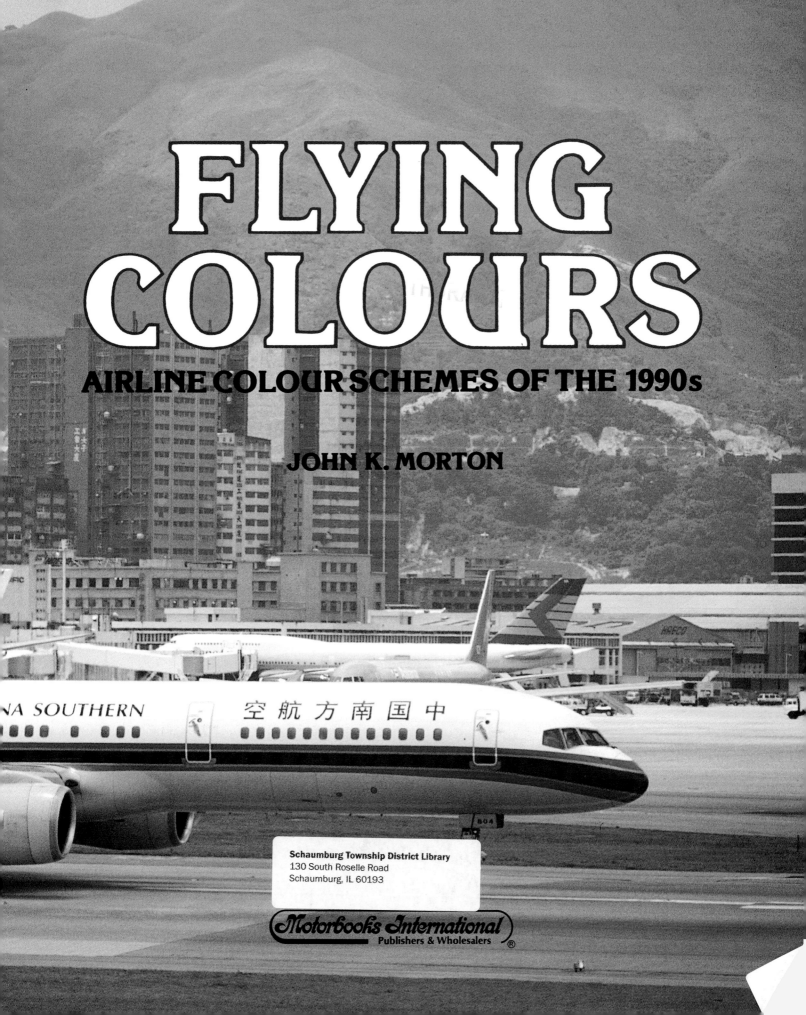

FLYING COLOURS

AIRLINE COLOUR SCHEMES OF THE 1990s

JOHN K. MORTON

空航方南国中

Motorbooks International
Publishers & Wholesalers ®

AUTHOR'S NOTE

In presenting *Flying Colours*, I have attempted to portray the vast and varied range of colours to be seen on the world's aircraft. The majority of the photographs are of passenger-carrying aircraft which arrive and depart daily at destinations around the globe, and were taken by me using Kodachrome 25 film and selected from my ever-increasing collection of over 14,000 transparencies.

An airline's corporate image is very important and vast sums of money are paid to design studios and agencies by carriers anxious to keep in step with modern trends. Styles change very fast and it is obviously necessary to choose a livery that will not date too quickly.

A book of this nature cannot be produced without the help of the authorities, and due acknowledgement must be made to all who made the production of *Flying Colours* possible. I am extremely grateful for the assistance given to me by the Federal Airports' Corporation of Australia, in particular the staff at Brisbane airport; Phil Warwick and Barry Barford of Cairns Port Authority; Colin Jeeves and Jack Caine at Perth International airport; the Civil Aviation Administration of Costa Rica; the Airports Authority of Thailand; Richard Peacock of the Airport Authority of Washoe County and last, but by no means least, my friend of long standing, Ethel Pattison of Los Angeles International.

Most airports around the world provide facilities for the observer and it is hoped that these arrangements will continue long into the future.

Your interest in *Flying Colours* is appreciated and I trust you will obtain as much pleasure from looking through the pages as I had whilst photographing around the world.

This edition first published in 1994
by Motorbooks International,
Publishers & Wholesalers,
PO Box 2, 729 Prospect Avenue,
Osceola, WI 54020, USA.
Reprinted 1995.

© John K. Morton, 1994

Previously published by
Airlife Publishing Ltd.
Shrewsbury, England, 1994

Motorbooks International books are also available at discounts in bulk quantity for industrial sales-promotional use. For details write to Special Sales Manager at the publisher's address.

Library of Congress Cataloging-in-Publication Data
Morton, John K.
    Flying colors / John K. Morton.
        p.   cm.
    Includes index.
    ISBN 0-87938-903-6
    1. Airplanes – Identification marks.
    2. Transport planes – Decoration.
    3. Aeronautics, Commercial – History.
    I. Title.
    TL603.M673   1994
    387.7'3340423'0275 – dc20   93-46379
                                        CIP

Printed and bound in Singapore
by Kyodo Printing Co. (S'pore) Pte Ltd.

Contents

SOUTH AND CENTRAL AMERICA

Following privatisation of the airline, Mexicana began a complete change of image incorporating a new livery theme. As aircraft are repainted, a standard white overall finish will be applied to its fleet with fuselage titles and individual tail colours in up to nineteen variations depicting Mexico's history.

McDonnell Douglas DC-10 N1004A illustrates the carrier's original livery and is seen about to depart Miami in December 1988, whilst the other three pictures featured in the spread show the new Mexicana image applied to their recently delivered Airbus A320s, also photographed at Miami in January 1992.

Aero Peru – Faucett are two airlines based in Peru and for a period of around four months, commencing mid-December 1991, combined their capacity on the Lima-Miami route. As a result Lockheed L1011 Tri-Star OB1455 received dual titles as illustrated in this December 1991 picture at Miami. The Aero Peru lettering was removed at the end of March 1992 and the aircraft is now to be seen bearing only Faucett titles.

Taca International Airlines is a Central American airline with its base in San Salvador. International passenger services are provided with its all-jet fleet of Boeing 737 and 767 aircraft. The same livery is applied to both types of aircraft as shown in these photographs taken at Miami. In December 1989, 767 N767TA, configured to all economy class layout, comes in to land on runway 30, whilst in December 1990, 737 N236TA, also with all economy class seating, lands on the same runway. N767TA is photographed again in January 1991 about to start its take-off roll departing to San Salvador on its daily flight.

Overleaf
Originally two separate airlines, TAN and SAHSA operated out of Honduras, both being founded in the 1940s. In the early part of 1989 the companies merged and their Boeing 737s appeared with TAN SAHSA titles on all aircraft. 200 Series HR-TNR, aptly named *Honduras*, was about to leave Miami for Tegucigalpa when photographed in December 1990.

In 1987 Ladeco were still flying in the original colours of red, yellow and white as seen on their Boeing 727 CC-CAO on finals to Miami in December of that year. This Chilean carrier currently operates an all jet fleet including BAe and Boeing aircraft although the Boeing 737 300 series CC-CYE, illustrated in the company's new livery, introduced in the summer of 1990, photographed about to depart Miami on the morning flight to Santiago in December of that year no longer operates this service, having been returned to the leasing company.

With its headquarters in San José, Costa Rica, Lacsa provide scheduled services to South, North and Central American destinations. Its daily flights to Miami are operated by their leased Airbus A320s of which the airline currently has five in the fleet. In December 1990 N482GX is seen about to depart Miami for San José with the early afternoon flight, whilst on the following day the same aircraft is about to touch down at Miami airport with the midday arrival from the Costa Rican capital.

Ecuatoriana still has, in the author's opinion, one of the best airline liveries to be seen. With its headquarters in Quito, Ecuador, the airline has now added two Airbus A310s to its fleet of Boeing 707s and one McDonnell Douglas DC-10. The A310s are used extensively on passenger services to North American destinations with daily flights to Miami. New York flights are performed by the DC-10. Prior to the introduction of the Airbus A310s, flights to Guayaquil and Quito were still being operated with 707 equipment and HC-BHY, shown turning on to runway 9L at Miami, is about to depart to Ecuador in December 1990. The airline commenced flights with A310s in October 1991 and HC-BRA is about to land at Miami in December of that year.

Several American airlines still utilise Boeing 707s as pure freighters and Lan Chile, the Chilean airline, currently has three examples included in its fleet. The livery of the aircraft is similar in all respects to the airline's passenger-carrying planes apart from the addition of the 'CARGO' inscription on the fuselage. Illustrated is CC-CER, which, like the other freight-carrying 707s were converted from regular passenger airliners, this one having previously flown in the ownership of Trans World Airlines.

Aviateca, the Central American airline is based in Guatemala City and currently has a fleet consisting entirely of Boeing 737s. Scheduled services are provided within Central America and points in North America. Its new livery shown on one of its 300 series 737s N75356, seen landing at Miami in December 1990, was introduced following the privatisation of the airline at the beginning of that year. This aircraft was subsequently returned to a leasing company and replaced by another 300 series aircraft.

Copa is a Panamanian airline, founded in 1947, which relies on its fleet of Boeing 737s to perform its passenger and freight services, originally contained within Central and South America. Upon the suspension of operations by Air Panama at the beginning of 1990, the Copa colours began to appear in North America when the airline replaced Air Panama on flights to Miami. In December 1990 HP-1163-CMP is about to land at the Southern Florida city after completing its journey from Panama.

Founded in 1919 and based in Colombia, Avianca operates an all-jet fleet of aircraft, and added Boeing 767 extended range models to its fleet in 1990. At the time of writing two examples were in use, both operating non-stop services from the country's capital Bogota to New York and Miami. One of the airline's 767s N985AN is seen arriving arriving at Miami in December 1990.

For the enthusiast looking for scheduled flights aboard a 1943 vintage Douglas DC-3 Dakota, Costa Rica is the place to head for. Daily flights from Juan Santamaria International Airport, San José, to seven destinations within Costa Rica are provided by Sansa, a subsidiary of the country's national carrier Lacsa. The photograph of DC-3 TI-SAG was taken at San José airport in April 1992 whilst awaiting passengers for its next short hop.

Based in Medellin, Colombia, Sam Colombia provides freight and passenger services mostly within South and Central America. Photographed at San José airport in April 1992 is one of the company's Boeing 727s HK-1271 which is seen about to depart on the 0900 hours flight to San Andres and Bogota. The entire fleet of Sam consists of 727s and HK-1271 is the only combi version.

Economy class seating is provided on all aircraft of Saeta, the Quito-based South American airline. Operating Boeing 707s and 727s, the airline has more recently taken delivery of an Airbus A310. Photographed in January 1992 is one of the carrier's 727s HC-BRG arriving at Miami operating the daily one-stop flight from Quito. After one and three-quarter hours on the ground the tri-jet will taxi to the runway for its take-off and return to Ecuador. This is a full day's work for the 727, having departed Quito at 0830, it will not touch down at its home base until 2100.

EUROPE

The regular 'Flying Colours' of British Airways, the British flag-carrier, are shown here carried on Boeing 737 G-BGDJ seen taxying from its stand at Düsseldorf in October 1985, and again on two of the airline's 757s operating shuttle flights out of London Heathrow in April 1990. In an attempt to persuade passengers to take to the air again following the conflict in the Gulf in January 1991, the airline introduced 'The World's Biggest Offer' to the general public and gave away 50,000 free tickets for seats on all its international flights taken on 23 April 1991. Passengers already holding reservations on that day were given free tickets to be used at a later date. Certain aircraft carried additional 'The World's Biggest Offer' titles applied to the fuselage, which are shown on Boeing 747 series 400 G-BNLS arriving at Hong Kong in May 1991 operating Speedbird flight 027 non-stop service from London Heathrow.

Often described as being the World's most beautiful airliner, Concorde can always make heads turn when arriving or departing at airports around the world. Twenty of these machines were built, and the only other airline operating services with them is Air France. Heads turn as one of those in the British Airways fleet crosses the threshold at Miami airport in January 1987. This was a continuing service of the London-Washington flight with the Washington-Miami and *vice-versa* sectors operating subsonic. The American portion of the service no longer operates.

Excalibur is a new British holiday airline which commenced operations on 1 May 1992 with a fleet of three Airbus A320s, the first United Kingdom charter company to operate the type. The three twin-jet aircraft are based at London Gatwick and Manchester and it is at the latter airport where G-KMAM was photographed in May 1992 about to depart to a Mediterranean destination with a charter flight. Services will operate from most of the United Kingdom regional airports to the holiday destinations of Europe, Egypt and West Africa.

Based in Luton, Monarch is another of the United Kingdom's inclusive tour and worldwide charter airlines. The company was formed in 1967 and currently has a fleet of Boeing 737s and 757s along with four Airbus A300s, the latter type entering service in 1990 and 1991. Boeing 757 G-MONC was photographed on finals to the island of Ibiza in August 1987. All Boeing 757s in Monarch's fleet are configured into economy class seating with spaces for 235 passengers.

Dan Air was founded in 1953 and derived its name from the holding company Davies and Newman, the London shipping company. The airline was one of the major inclusive-tour charter operators in the UK, flying from the main British airports to numerous holiday destinations around Europe. Dan Air also provided scheduled services utilizing its fleet of propeller-driven and jet aircraft. Spain is a very popular destination for the British holidaymaker and the airline served many of that country's resorts, both on the mainland and the islands, Ibiza being one of the island destinations. It is at this island that Boeing 737 G-BLDE was seen about to the return to the United Kingdom in August 1987.

Dan Air ran into financial difficulties at the end of October 1992 and was taken over by British Airways when the airline paid a sum of £1 to assume overall control. Dan Air's previous routes were re-shaped, several of their Boeing 737s re-painted in the new owner's colours and all of their previous original charter operations suspended.

A scene repeated daily at London's Gatwick airport although not necessarily in the same sequence. Long-haul 747s, having travelled half-way around the world overnight, arrive mid-morning at their stands at the South terminal and depart later to various worldwide destinations.

Aer Lingus, the Anglicised version of Aer Loingeas (meaning 'air fleet'), are based in Dublin and operate an all-Boeing fleet of aircraft. Founded by the Irish Government in 1936, the national airline of the Republic of Ireland naturally makes full use of the Irish Shamrock as part of its identity. This forms the design applied to the tail of the company's aircraft, together with the distinctive emerald green. Both international and regional flights are provided by Aer Lingus from Dublin, Shannon and Cork to points within Europe and the United States, including a comprehensive service between Dublin and Manchester. It is at the latter city where the first flight of the day is seen arriving, operated by one of the carrier's Boeing 737s.

Air UK Leisure was formed in 1987 as a subsidiary of Air UK to provide charter flights from United Kingdom airports to European holiday destinations. One of the airline's series 300 Boeing 737s G-UKLD is seen arriving at Manchester in July 1991 whilst operating a summer charter flight. Air UK Leisure has a fleet of this type of aircraft and took delivery of the Boeing 767 type during 1992.

Viva, the Spanish leisure airline and subsidiary of Iberia, the national airline of Spain, operate a fleet of Boeing 737 series 300s from their Palma base. Formed jointly by Iberia and the German airline Lufthansa in the early part of 1988, Viva provides scheduled services to a variety of European destinations. Arriving at London Heathrow's Terminal 2 whilst operating the carrier's weekly flight from Gran Canaria in June 1992 is EC-FLF, shown in the airline's attractive Spanish-style livery.

BEA at one time was carried on aircraft of the British flag-carrier British European Airways before its merger with British Overseas Airways Corporation. Now, the initials BEA are carried on Birmingham European Airways fleet of aircraft of which BAC 1-11 G-AWBL is one of nine aircraft flown by the company which is based in the United Kingdom's second city — Birmingham. The twin jet is seen as it is pushed back from the terminal at Birmingham International Airport in July 1992, operating a scheduled flight to a destination in Europe. Birmingham European merged with Brymon Airways at the beginning of 1993 and BEA became to be known as Brymon European Airways.

Lufthansa, the German flag-carrier with a fleet of over 250 aircraft operate worldwide services. The airline expects to be the first to operate revenue-earning services with the new Airbus A340 four-engined jet. The basic livery of Lufthansa is over 20 years old and during 1988 several experiments were made to revise the design. A new scheme did eventually appear, albeit the only significant change being the removal of the cheat line originally displayed. The current livery is illustrated here on Boeing 747 D-ABYP arriving at Los Angeles in August 1990 after completing its non-stop flight of 5,786 miles from Frankfurt.

Air Berlin was set up on 1978 to operate passenger charter services from Berlin's Tegel airport to Spain and the Mediterranean. The carrier commenced operations using Boeing 707 aircraft obtaining four examples from TWA, but these were replaced with a single Boeing 737-300 series during the early part of 1986. The livery of the airline was changed upon the introduction of this aircraft and is still in use today. American registered N67AB is about to depart Palma for Berlin in May 1986.

Until recently, LTU, the German airline, concentrated on inclusive tour and charter operations utilising its all Lockheed L1011 fleet. The distinctive colours of the airline could be seen in a number of locations. More recently the company applied to provide scheduled services and these commenced at the beginning of 1990. Additional aircraft were brought into the fleet which now include the McDonnell Douglas MD-11, and orders have been placed for the Airbus A330. One of the airline's scheduled flights is the thrice weekly service from the company's base in Düsseldorf to Miami and it is at the sunshine state city where L1011 D-AERT was photographed in January 1988 about to depart for Germany.

Founded in 1969, Maersk Air commenced services at the beginning of 1970 originally providing charter and inclusive tour flights from its base in Copenhagen. Scheduled services are now also operated by the airline to destinations within Scandinavia together with international flights to the United Kingdom. When operating a charter flight, Boeing 737 series 300 OY-MMN was about to depart from the island of Ibiza in August 1987.

Norway Airlines was formed in 1987, commencing services with two Boeing 737-300s operating inclusive tour flights to the Canary Islands and the Mediterranean. The company now lease out their two 737s and utilise McDonnell Douglas MD-83 and -87 aircraft to provide its services. Boeing LN-NOS in the colours of Norway Airlines was on summer lease to the British carrier Britannia when photographed at London's Gatwick airport in June 1988. The aircraft remained in the livery of its owner whilst flying for Britannia. Norway Airlines entered into voluntary liquidation in October 1992 and attempted to restart operations with financial assistance provided by the Dutch airline Air Holland. However, this rescue bid failed.

Conair, the Scandinavian charter operator, was founded in 1963 and at one time had its fleet made up entirely of Boeing 720s. Its present fleet is now completely Airbus aircraft comprising A300s and A320s, configured into all economy class seating. Delivery of the A320s was made towards the end of 1991 and the airline immediately put them into service on their long distance charter operations. Airbus A320 OY-CNG is seen at Ford Lauderdale, Florida, in April 1992. The aircraft arrived from Denmark and departed after only 50 minutes on the ground.

Time Air Sweden was a Stockholm-based charter operator which started services in the spring of 1991 with two Boeing 737-200 series. A McDonnell Douglas DC-8 was leased during the winter 1991/92 to provide additional capacity for Swedish tour operators. Boeing 737 SE-DLG was seen arriving at Ibiza airport in July 1992, a leased aircraft, having previously flown in the ownership of America West Airlines. Air Sweden ran into financial difficulties in February 1993, and its three aircraft were repossessed.

Opposite
Air Toulouse International operate only Caravelles and have a fleet of three. This relatively small airline, founded in 1969 and with a staff of 40, operate flights in and around Europe from their base in the south of France. Frankfurt/Main ground staff are assisting the 1964-built Caravelle F-BMKS to prepare for take-off in this August 1992 shot.

Brussels-based Air Belgium was formed in 1979 to provide charter flights for tour companies. Its present fleet consists of two Boeing 737s and one Boeing 757, all painted in the current livery of the airline which was introduced in 1982, replacing the black and white colour scheme previously employed. Boeing 737 OO-ILH has just arrived at its stand at Ibiza airport as the sun is about to set.

Opposite
Swissair, the airline of Switzerland. The huge size of the winglets fitted to the wing tips of the McDonnell Douglas MD-11 aircraft are clearly shown on Swissair's first example of the type to be delivered. HB-IWA has just been pushed back from the gate at Bangkok International Airport in August 1991 at the start of its continuing flight from Zürich.

Yugoslav Airlines, the national carrier of Yugoslavia, was formed by the government in 1947 to provide both European and worldwide flights. Its long haul services are operated by the company's three McDonnell Douglas DC-10s, whilst McDonnell Douglas DC-9s and Boeing 727 and 737 aircraft are utilised on European sectors. Boeing 737 series 300 YU-ANH was arriving at London Heathrow Terminal 2 when photographed in July 1990. The title Yugoslavia Airlines appears on the other side of the fuselage. Reports suggest that the airline will be renamed 'Aeroput' in the future.

Originally known as Turk Hava Yollari, the Turkish national carrier changed its name towards the end of 1989 and is now known simply as Turkish Air. At the same time, the company introduced a new colour scheme which is shown on McDonnell Douglas DC-9 TC-JAK proceeding to its allocated stand at Frankfurt/Main airport in August 1992. This design was finally adopted after several other experiments.

Shown in the original colours and bearing the titles Turk Hava Yollari, this May 1986 picture at Frankfurt illustrates well the airline's image change. Airbus A310 TC-JCS was operating a scheduled flight to Istanbul.

Istanbul Airlines, based in Istanbul, took to the air in 1985. Caravelles and Boeing 727s and 737s make up its fleet of fourteen aircraft which are employed on the company's scheduled services to various European cities together with airports within Turkey. Also photographed at Frankfurt/Main is Boeing 727 TC-AFR seen arriving on a late afternoon service.

Formed in 1990 jointly by Turkish Airlines and Lufthansa, Sun Express is based in Antalya, Turkey, and has a fleet of three Boeing 737 series 300s. This charter airline operates holiday flights from Turkish resorts to German destinations, and TC-SUN was on such a flight when photographed in August 1992. The location is again Frankfurt/Main.

Airlines quite often delay the presentation of a revised or new livery until new aircraft on order are delivered, taking the opportunity of combining the introduction of a new airliner and new colours at the same time. Tunis Air was no exception when their stylish new livery was introduced upon the delivery of their Airbus A320s in the summer of 1990. Airbus A320 TS-IMC was the second of the type to be delivered to Tunis Air and was photographed at Frankfurt/Main in August 1992 after completing the 915-mile journey from Tunis.

Lauda Air was formed in 1979 by the world champion racing driver Nikki Lauda, initially as a charter operator and later also as a scheduled carrier. The present fleet of this Austrian company includes both Boeing 737s and 767s, the latter type being employed on scheduled services to Bangkok, Sydney, Melbourne, Hong Kong and Miami from their Vienna base. Series 300 extended range 767 OE-LAV, aptly named *Johann Strauss*, has just arrived at Bangkok airport in August 1991. The Boeing will stay on the ground around one hour before continuing its journey to Hong Kong.

Overleaf
The tiny island of Malta, situated in the Mediterranean, formed its own airline in 1973 to provide scheduled passenger and cargo services. Its current fleet consists of Boeing 737s and Airbus A320s which are employed on the company's services within Europe and the Mediterranean. A four times per week Malta-Frankfurt service is currently operated and both types of aircraft are used on these flights. Boeing 737 9H-ABC was the aircraft in use when the midday flight arrived at the gate at Frankfurt/Main in August 1992.

Largest of the Danish charter operators, Sterling, began operations in 1962 under the ownership of the country's major travel company. Passenger charters to worldwide holiday destinations are operated from their Copenhagen base, and the company recently added the Boeing 757 extended range aircraft to their fleet. Boeing 727 OY-SBO was operating a return charter flight to Denmark; photographed when about to depart Ibiza in August 1987.

Originally known as Alisarda, the company changed its name to Meridiana, its sister company based in Palma, to provide scheduled services alongside its previous charter operations. Scheduled services commenced in September 1991 and operate out of Florence, Italy. Services to major European destinations are provided using a fleet of BAe 146 and McDonnell Douglas DC-9 and MD-82 aircraft. DC-9 I-SMEE was being employed on a Frankfurt-Florence service when photographed about to leave the German city in August 1992.

DOWN UNDER

One of the world's oldest airlines, the title Qantas is derived from Queensland and Northern Territory Aerial Services. Its long range fleet of aircraft are entirely Boeing machines of 747 and 767 examples. Included in the fleet are two Special Performance 747s referred to as 'SPs', one of which is VH-EAB seen arriving at Perth in April 1991. The kangaroo is Australia's national symbol and it appears on the tails of both Qantas and Australian aircraft.

The airline began operating the 767 during the mid-1980s and are due to accept delivery of their last ordered models in late 1994. When these are delivered from Boeing, the airline will have twenty-two of the Seattle-manufactured twin jets in their fleet. One of their 1990-delivered aircraft VH-OGH is seen departing Cairns in Northern Queensland in August 1991.

As well as the two 747SP aircraft, the Qantas fleet also included thirty-one regular 747 models in the 200, 300 and 400 series. VH-EBQ is one of the carrier's 200 series Jumbos and was photographed about to touch down on the runway at Sydney airport in April 1989.

Overleaf
The skyline and skyscrapers of the city of Sydney provide a very pleasing background to Boeing 747 series 300 VH-EBY as it is towed from the international terminal to the Qantas maintenance hangars in April 1989.

Compass Airlines was the first Australian airline to introduce passenger services after deregulation, commencing operations at the end of 1990. Flights were provided to both East and West coasts of Australia using leased Airbus A300 aircraft. After only one year of operations however, the airline folded due to heavy losses and its aircraft were returned to the leasing companies. A new airline retaining the original name was formed which began services in September 1992 with a small fleet of McDonnell Douglas MD-80s. The second start-up of the airline also proved to be unsuccessful, and Compass discontinued flights in March 1993. Prior to the first curtailment of services, Airbus A300 VH-YMJ is seen in April 1991 arriving at Perth with the morning flight from Sydney.

Domestic flights within Australia are provided by one of the country's other airlines. Australian, as it is now known, was originally named Trans Australian Airlines when it came into being in 1946. Its modern fleet consists of Boeing 737s, 727s and Airbus A300s. One of the company's 737s VH-TAF, a series 300 model, was about to depart Sydney when photographed in April 1989.

Boeing 737 series 300 VH-TAK named
Daring is seen at its stand at Perth airport
receiving passengers for its next service
and awaiting push-back.

Opposite
The tail markings of Australian are clearly
shown in this picture of *Daring*.
Immediately behind the 737 can be seen
Ansett Australia, one of Australia's other
domestic airlines. Australian was
purchased by Qantas at the end of 1992
and combined services. Until this time
Qantas had no domestic routes.

Slightly larger than Australian in terms of aircraft numbers, Ansett was originally called Ansett Airlines of Australia. A domestic service linking several towns and cities throughout the Australian continent is provided by its jet fleet. Photographed at Melbourne in April 1989 VH-RME, one of the airline's Boeing 767s, shows the original shooting stars motif carried on the tails of Ansett's aircraft.

A close-up of Hotel-Yankee-Foxtrot's tail, together with the same motif carried on one of Ansett's Fokker F28s completes the picture.

Towards the end of 1990, the company changed its name yet again, now to become known as Ansett Australia. To celebrate the deregulation of carriers in the country, the airline unveiled a new livery replacing the shooting star tail motif with a plain blue tail containing white stars and part of the Australian flag. The new colours are shown carried on Airbus A320 (*Skystar*) VH-HYF photographed at Perth in April 1991.

With a small fleet of aircraft, East-West, founded in New South Wales in 1947, provides feeder services within Australia. The two illustrations shown here are of aircraft no longer in the company's fleet, its present aircraft consisting of BAe 146s and leased Boeing 727. In April 1989, whilst still operating for East-West, Fokker F28 VH-EWD was photographed arriving at Sydney airport's domestic terminal.

East-West operated Boeing 737-300 series G-PATE on behalf of the Queensland Government during the early part of 1990 and was photographed in April of that year at Brisbane airport whilst being loaded and prepared for departure.

Opposite
Solomon Airlines was founded in 1968 and is based in Honiara in the Solomon Islands. The company operate only the Boeing 737 on its international services to New Zealand, Australia and Vanuatu, the island situated in the Coral Sea. All of the other airline's services are provided by the company's Twin Otter and Islander aircraft. A weekly service from Honiara to Queensland is offered by Solomon, and Boeing 737 H4-SAL was photographed taxying to the runway at Cairns in August 1991 at the commencement of the return journey to its base.

Air Pacific — the national carrier of Fiji was founded in 1951. The airline operate their international services with leased airliners, and Boeing 747 VH-EBJ, shown in the full colours of the airline at Sydney's international terminal in April 1990, was on lease from the Australian airline Qantas.

71

P2-ANG was delivered to Air Niugini at the end of 1990 and the Airbus A310 is used to provide international flights from Port Moresby to Australia, Singapore, Manila and Hong Kong. The illustration shows the twin jet about to depart Cairns in August 1991 on a return flight to Port Moresby. Air Niugini was formed in 1973 following Papua-New Guinea's independence from Australia. Together with the A310, the airline's fleet is made up of Dash 7s and Fokker F28 aircraft.

Air Nauru, owned by the Government of the Republic of Nauru, began operations in 1970. The island of Nauru is situated in the South West Pacific ocean and the airline operates all its flights utilising its fleet of Boeing 737s. The author was anxious to add a photograph of one of the carrier's aircraft into his collection, and succeeded in shooting C2-RN3 in the late evening light arriving at Melbourne on the once-a-week flight from Nauru in April 1989.

AFRICA/MIDDLE EAST/INDIAN SUB-CONTINENT

In October 1989, Air India unveiled its new livery to the aviation world which was applied to its aircraft when re-painting became necessary. Boeing 747 VT-EBE, parked at its stand at London Heathrow's Terminal 3 in May 1990, illustrates the distinctive red sash and golden sun which formed the design of the tail. Recent reports suggest however, that Air India will revert to its original livery which appears on the 747 parked immediately behind Echo-Bravo-Echo.

Indian Airlines, the country's domestic carrier, operate from their base in New Delhi with Boeing 737 and Airbus A300 and A320 aircraft. All of their A320s were grounded following the crash of VT-EPN at Bangalore in February 1990 but the type are now fully operational again. Operating the service to Calcutta on an August afternoon in 1991 is VT-EPE, one of the carrier's A320s, which has managed to depart Bangkok airport between the heavy showers.

East West Airlines is a new Indian carrier
established in 1992 and based in Bombay.
The airline took to the air on 28 February
of that year with services from Bombay to
Mangalore and Cochin. Leased Boeing
737s are employed by this domestic carrier
and additional jets and Fokker Friendship
F27s have been brought into the fleet to
provide services to new destinations
including Goa, Jaipur and Trivandrum.
Boeing 737 VT-EWC is one of three of the
Seattle-based manufacturer's twin jets with
which East West started operations and is
seen on final approach to Goa airport,
completing the hour-long flight from
Bombay in October 1992.

Emirates is a recently formed company founded in 1985 and based in Dubai. A comprehensive service is provided by the airline from its international airport in the United Arab Emirates, with a fleet of Boeing 727 and Airbus A300 and A310 jets. A thrice-weekly flight from Dubai to Bangkok and Manila was in operation when Airbus A300-600R A6-EKE was photographed in March 1991, seen under the control of the push-back tractor about to depart Bangkok on the second stage of its 4,400-mile journey to the Philippines capital.

Boeing 747SP EP-IAA is one of four special performance jumbos flown by The Airline of The Islamic Republic of Iran — Iran Air. Originally founded in 1947, the airline was reformed in 1962 by the government of Iran wishing to provide a more modern and efficient airline to give a better worldwide image. Both passenger and freight services are operated by the company's all-jet fleet, and the illustration of the SP shown here was taken at Frankfurt/Main in October 1985.

Ghana Airways was formed by the government of this West African country formally known as the Gold Coast. Based in Accra, the entire fleet of the airline totals four aircraft, one of which being McDonnell Douglas DC-10 9G-ANA here seen departing London's Gatwick airport in May 1986. The airliner has been in the fleet of Ghana Airways since being delivered new from the manufacturer at the beginning of 1983, and currently makes three flights per week from Accra to London.

Originally known as Alia, Royal Jordanian from the Kingdom of Jordan, introduced its new and current livery during 1986. The titling appears both in English and Arabic, but no further use of the earlier title — Alia, is apparent. The airline's earlier title was in fact the name of King Hussein's daughter. French-registered Airbus A310 F-ODVE named *Princess Iman* was operating a scheduled flight to Amman when captured by the camera at Frankfurt/Main in October 1987.

Formerly known as East Pakistan, the country was renamed Bangladesh in 1971 after a nine-month-long war of independence. Bangladesh Airlines was formed in January 1972 and named Bangladesh Biman operating out of its base in Dhaka. All of the company's long haul flights are scheduled for DC-10 operation, and one of the airline's fleet of four, S2-ACO, is seen at Bangkok in April 1991 being pushed back from the terminal.

Formed in 1950 and owned by a consortium of countries including Bahrain, Qatar, Oman and the United Arab Emirates, Gulf Air operate within the Gulf area together with scheduled flights to Europe and the Far East. Its modern jet fleet includes aircraft from the three main manufacturers, Boeing, Lockheed and Airbus. Boeing 767 A40-GG, an extended range model, is receiving the attention of the Bangkok ground staff after being pushed back in April 1991.

It was not until the end of 1971 that this airline became known as Egyptair. Prior to this date the company, based at Cairo International airport, was named United Arab Airlines. Scheduled domestic and international flights are provided by the airline, including a Cairo to Düsseldorf once-weekly service. When operating this flight in October 1985, the company utilised one of their A300 aircraft, and SU-GAA is pictured arriving at the German city. *Isis*, as the Airbus is named, no longer flies for Egyptair and the service is now being operated by Boeing 767s, delivered to the airline in 1989.

American-registered McDonnell Douglas DC-10 N3016Z has been in the fleet of Zambia Airways since its delivery to the airline in July 1984. It is the company's only wide body aircraft, which was photographed in October 1987 about to depart Frankfurt/Main airport. The airline, having being founded in 1967, is owned by the government of this African country.

THE FAR EAST

Eva Air, the Chinese carrier, was formed in 1989 and has its base on the island of Taiwan. The airline commenced services in July 1991 with two leased Boeing 767 extended-range aircraft operating from Taiwan to Bangkok, Singapore, Seoul and Jakarta. Further deliveries of 767s have been made to the airline who have also placed orders for future deliveries of the McDonnell Douglas MD-11. Eva Air took delivery of the first of eight ordered Boeing 747 series 400 long-range airliners in November 1992 which was placed into service on the Taiwan-Vienna-London route. B-16602, the second of Eva Air's Boeing 767s to be acquired, had just arrived at Bangkok from Taiwan in August 1991 when photographed taxying to the terminal.

Asiana is the newest of the Korean airlines, having been formed in 1988. Based in Seoul, the carrier commenced operations using Boeing 737s on domestic routes and later introduced 767s to Hong Kong and Singapore flights. Longer international services are now provided, and Boeing 747 series 400 jumbos are operating the services. Boeing 767 HL7264 has just left the gate at Hong Kong and prepares to depart for Seoul in June 1991.

The government-owned airline of Vietnam was originally named Hang Khong Vietnam when formed in 1976 and retained this title, which appeared on the carrier's aircraft, until being named Vietnam Airlines in the summer of 1990. Until this time, the livery carried by the predominantly Soviet fleet was very similar to that of the Russian airline Aeroflot. Upon the change of name a new colour scheme was introduced which is illustrated on Tupolev 134A VN-A106 photographed at Bangkok in April 1991.

Overleaf
The vastness of the People's Republic of China and the huge distances within the country made it necessary for the national airline – CAAC – to operate in a similar way to that of Russia's airline Aeroflot, prior to the Soviet Union becoming a Commonwealth of Independent States. Until that time, the Soviet airline operated all services within the USSR which were later to be split into divisions, each division having its own title. This system was adopted by the Chinese carrier in the late 1980s when several regional airlines were given self-management but still operated under the direct leadership of the CAAC. As the regional airlines became self-managed they introduced their own colour schemes and replaced CAAC titles with their own. China Southern, operating out of Guangzhou (Canton), was one of the carriers, and one of their Boeing 757s, B2804, is seen gathering speed as it rushes down the runway at Hong Kong at the start of its one-hour-long flight to Guangzhou.

Air China is another of China's regional airlines which has adopted its own colour scheme since replacing the original CAAC titling. More international services are provided by Air China than other carriers within the leadership of CAAC with regular flights to the United States, Europe and Canada. For these services Air China operates a fleet of Boeing 747s in three versions, Special Performance, 200 series with side cargo doors, and long-range 400 series. Air China International was formed in 1988 and has its headquarters in Beijing. Boeing 767 B-2556, a long range version aircraft delivered new to the airline in February 1989, has just arrived at Hong Kong airport in May 1991.

When China Eastern appeared on the
scene, it was still possible to see CAAC
titles carried on aircraft which had earlier
passed over to the now self-managed
group. Not until aircraft were taken out of
service for overhaul were new colours
applied. China Eastern has its base in
Shanghai from where it operates its
passenger and freight services. It had been
quite a miserable day at Hong Kong in
April 1990 when Airbus A300 B-2308 had
arrived earlier in the afternoon. However,
as the clouds cleared and the sun got lower
in the sky, a brilliant evening ensued and
the Airbus departed in full sun.

Thai International — the flag-carrier of Thailand, was formed by the country's government in 1959. The airline currently operates a comprehensive route system connecting Bangkok with major cities in Europe and throughout Australia and the Far East. Thai's extremely attractive livery was introduced in 1975 and features the orchid, the national flower of Thailand, together with the colours which one associates with the country — magenta, gold and purple. The airline recently took delivery of the long-range 400 series Boeing 747 which are used on non-stop international services. HS-TGJ is making its way to the terminal at Bangkok airport in August 1991.

Boeing 737 HS-TBE had arrived on the same runway just ahead of the jumbo as the heavens opened, bringing a torrential downpour during the oppressive rainy season.

This must be the plane-spotters' delight. Airbuses in a row, parked, and awaiting their next duties, are each prepared and cleaned away from the terminal. As departure time approaches, the Thai tow-truck will slowly move the airliners to their respective gates.

1991 was 'Visit Indonesia Year', and the country's national airline Garuda took this message to most parts of the world, inviting holidaymakers to enjoy the various attractions that Indonesian islands have to offer. Garuda provide a comprehensive service linking these islands, together with connections to the capital Jakarta and points throughout the Far East and Europe. McDonnell Douglas DC-10 PK-GID is one of seven series 30 aircraft flown by the airline which are included in a fleet of over 60 airliners of other types. The present livery was introduced in 1985 replacing the company's previous colours of red and white. Garuda was taking its country's message to Australia when the DC-10 was photographed at Perth in April 1991. The tractor was about to detach after push-back.

The tail motif depicting a bird is illustrated on a Garuda Airbus A300 parked immediately behind a SAS Boeing 767 at Singapore in April 1991.

In 1948, Korean National Airlines was formed by the government in power at the time, later to become Korean Air in 1962 and establish itself as the South Korean flag-carrier. When established, the colours of Korean Air were red, white and blue which remained with the airline until their revised livery appeared in 1984. McDonnell Douglas, Boeing and Airbus Industry aircraft are included in the Korean Air fleet which provides services to Europe and the United States, along with destinations in the Far East. A close-up of the tail motif is shown on a Boeing 747, whilst newly-delivered McDonnell Douglas MD-11 HL7372, about to roll down Hong Kong's runway in May 1991, shows off the livery in its entirety.

The Philippine Islands forming the Republic of the Philippines are situated 500 miles off the South East coast of Asia, bounded on the east by the Pacific and by the China Sea on the west. Its national airline now wholly-owned by the government, was originally formed in 1941, but due to the Japanese invasion during World War Two, a full service was not provided until 1946. Almost fifty years later Philippine Airlines has emerged to become a leading carrier operating a modern fleet of aircraft. Long-haul services are operated by the company's Boeing 747s and McDonnell Douglas DC-10s, whilst Airbus and BAe 1-11 jets are used on regional and domestic flights. The airline's current colours were unveiled at the end of 1986 and supercedes the previous, which were basically the same apart from the revised tail livery, which now includes a golden sun burst. DC-10 RPC2003 has completed its push-back operation and is ready to depart Melbourne airport in April 1989.

The aircraft carries the 1986 livery. A close-up of the 'bursting sun' design on the tail of the DC-10 shows clearly the make-up of the design.

Hong Kong-based Cathay Pacific, one of the major carriers in South-East Asia, was formed following the Second World War and commenced scheduled services in 1948. Only wide-bodied aircraft are included in the company's fleet which currently fly Lockheed L1011s and Boeing 747s, exclusively powered by Rolls-Royce engines, to destinations around the world. Bangkok is one of thirty-eight cities in twenty-five countries served by Cathay, where Lockheed TriStar VR-HOK is seen in April 1991 about to depart on a non-stop Hong Kong service.

Singapore Airlines has achieved worldwide recognition over the years for top quality in-flight service and attention by their famous 'Singapore Girls' flight attendants. The airline was established in 1972 succeeding Malaysia-Singapore Airlines and Malaysia Airlines which were formed during the days of British Colonial rule. Singapore Airlines quickly captured a large share of the market it operated, and accordingly enlarged its fleet, which consists of only two types of aircraft — the Boeing 747 and Airbus A310. The carrier's 747s are in three varieties, 200 series, 300 series called BIG TOP, and the 400 series referred to as MEGATOP. The stylish yellow bird, which is a feature of Singapore Airlines colours, is carried on the tails of the aircraft, and repeated on the engine casings and winglets of the 747-400s. Airbus A310 9V-STM was operating a Singapore flight when photographed at Bangkok in April 1991.

The airline recently commenced one-stop
services from Singapore to Manchester,
and 9V-SKP, one of fourteen BIG TOPS, is
seen arriving at its destination early one
July morning in 1990.

Opposite
A more detailed illustration of the yellow
bird is shown on another A310 (the blue
section is not part of the livery — maybe
the aft rest room is equipped with blue
flush!)

All Nippon Airways, the Tokyo-based carrier, was formed in 1972 and is one of Japan's foremost airlines accepted as being the largest domestic carrier in the land operating various types of aircraft on these services, all of which are configured into economy class on their short-haul routes. Included in the domestic fleet are Boeing 747s, fitted with an incredible total of 569 seats. International flights are also flown by All Nippon and three classes are available on services to Europe and the United States. Daily flights from Tokyo to Hong Kong are operated by Lockheed TriStars and JA8521 was in use on the return service when photographed about to enter the Hong Kong runway in April 1990.

Associated with All Nippon Airways, Nippon Cargo Airlines was formed in 1978 as a pure freight-carrying airline. The colours are exactly the same as the passenger-carrying company albeit there are variations in the actual design. Nippon Cargo operate a fleet made up exclusively of Boeing 747 freighters, and the illustration shows one example of the fleet, JA8172, about to depart San Francisco in August 1990.

Hong Kong-based Dragonair was founded in 1985 and commenced services with Boeing 737 aircraft painted in a traditionally Chinese livery of orange and gold, incorporating a golden dragon on the aircraft's tail. The company continue to operate 737s, and added to the fleet in the summer of 1990 when an ex-Eastern Airlines Lockheed L1011 was put into service. Flights to mainland China and Nepal are provided by Dragonair, and the company recently added Hiroshima to their timetable, served three times per week by Boeing 737. On order are five Airbus A320s due for delivery in 1993, and it is reported that the introduction of these airliners will coincide with a new colour scheme. Shown in the current livery at Hong Kong in May 1991 is the ex-Eastern TriStar VR-HOD.

Not to be confused with mainland China, China Airlines is based in the Republic of China, originally called Formosa but now known as Taiwan. Its modern international airport, located in the country's capital Taipai, is named after the former President Chiang Kai-Shek, who left mainland China with his soldiers during the conflict with the communists in 1949. The title China Airlines appeared in 1960 after a period of being known as China Air Transport, at which time a programme of expansion followed. China Airlines now operate a modern jet fleet providing flights to many worldwide destinations. Included in the airline's fleet are Boeing 747-400s which were delivered at the beginning of 1990, B-192 was the second example to be delivered and was photographed arriving at Los Angeles International in August 1990 whilst only a few months old.

America West was formed in 1981 as a low fare airline offering scheduled services originally in the Western States of the US. Flights were started with a small number of Boeing 737s, and as the company progressed, more aircraft were added and their fleet now includes Airbus A320s and Boeing 747 and 757s, the former being utilised on the company's services to Honolulu. Flights throughout the continental United States are now made by America West. At the time of writing, the airline is under Chapter 11 Bankruptcy Protection to enable operations to continue. Boeing 737 N183AW is seen crossing one of the many taxiways at Los Angeles International airport in August 1990.

Boeing 737 N158AW is overnighting at Reno airport in July 1990. Several of the carrier's 737s arrive at the Nevada city in the early evening and position in readiness for the first flights the following morning.

Overleaf
American — one of the most well-known of the North American airlines, founded in 1934 and currently employing almost 100,000 staff. With a fleet in excess of 600 aircraft, American serves most cities in the United States and Europe and is constantly adding new routes to its already extensive network. Included in the airline's fleet are sixty-six Boeing 767 Luxury Liners of which N313AA is an extended range model. The twin jet is taxying at San Francisco airport in August 1990.

Originally known as Northwest Orient, the airline dropped the word 'Orient' in 1986 and is now known simply as Northwest. The airline has been flying for some considerable time, having been established in 1926 as Northwest Airways Inc. Its fleet now exceeds 400 jet passenger and cargo-carrying aircraft. One of the company's passenger jumbos N621US pictured in the revised livery of the airline has just arrived at London Gatwick after completing the daily flight from Minneapolis/St Paul in June 1991, whilst cargo version jumbo N617US, one of eight of Northwest's 747 freighters, was photographed at San Francisco airport in August 1990.

Sun Country Airlines is a Minneapolis/St Paul-based charter airline having been formed in 1983. Its main operations are providing passenger charters to points within North America, Mexico and the Caribbean with a fleet of Boeing 727s and McDonnell Douglas DC-10s, brightly painted in the company's red, orange and yellow livery. One of the main destinations is Las Vegas where the carrier brings gamblers eager to break the bank at the many casinos. It is at the Nevada resort where Boeing 727 N275AF was photographed in July 1988 about to take-off.

Another of the United States better-known airlines is Delta, which has transported millions of passengers since its formation in 1928. Until services to London and Europe were started in 1978/1979, Delta routes were concentrated on the Americas, Bermuda and Canada. Following the unfortunate demise of PanAm, Delta took over most of the remaining trans-Atlantic routes previously operated by Pan American and at the same time assumed their Frankfurt hub. Lockheed L1011 N756DR which came into the Delta fleet in 1985, is being pushed back from the gate at Frankfurt/Main in October 1989 prior to commencing a trans-Atlantic flight. The aircraft was delivered new to PanAm and was purchased by Delta before PanAm ceased services.

Delta also has a large fleet of Boeing 757s which operate the airline's North American services. The mighty Pratt & Whitney engines idle gently as N624DL pauses momentarily at the holding point of San Francisco airport runway.

Boeing 727 N8876Z photographed in December 1989 taxying for take-off from Fort Launderdale airport in the livery of Bahamasair was actually an Eastern Airlines aircraft on lease to the carrier. The 727 flew for Bahamasair for around six months, and operated daily flights from Florida to Grand Bahama.

Tower Air commenced services in 1982 and currently has an all-Boeing 747 fleet of twelve aircraft, all of which are configured into economy class seating. The carrier provides both charter and scheduled services from the Eastern seaboard of the USA to points in Europe and the Middle East. On final approach to Miami in December 1989, Boeing 747 N603FF bears the original livery of the airline, whilst the revised colours of Tower Air have been applied to Boeing 747 N604FF about to turn on to runway 12 at the same Florida city in December 1991.

US Air joined the ranks of other American airlines and has become one of the major carriers in North America. With transcontinental and trans-Atlantic services contained in their schedules, US Air aircraft are to be seen at both international and domestic airports. A subsidiary of US Air, Piedmont Airlines, was integrated into the US Air group in the summer of 1989, which, for a time, resulted in airliners carrying hybrid liveries. The airline now had a combined route system covering Canada, the United States and the United Kingdom. Boeing series 300 N573US originally flew with Piedmont Airlines and is seen in the hybrid livery referred to, whilst Boeing 737-300 N524AU carries the original US Air livery of 1988. BAe 146 N187US shows the latest colours of the airline currently in use. All the shots in this spread were taken at San Francisco airport in July 1990.

Comair is a regional airline which flies scheduled services in the mid-western United States. Commuter operations were started in 1977, and in the late summer of 1984 the company became involved with Delta Air Lines to provide feeder services to Delta's hub cities, whilst still retaining their own colours and identity. N179CA is one of forty Embraer 120T Brasilia aircraft included in Comair's fleet, and is seen about to depart Fort Lauderdale in December 1990.

Christmas Day in Miami and the airport is relatively quiet apart from the long-haul traffic bringing in the sun-seekers and holidaymakers, most of which will celebrate New Year on the beaches. Evergreen International operate a scheduled cargo service within America, and Boeing 727 N728EV has had a rest day. The setting sun brings life to the Evergreen colours as the 1966-built aircraft, which previously carried passengers, awaits its next assignment.

Boeing 707s, which were commonplace thirty years ago, are now quite rare. Most of the major airlines put them into passenger service on trans-Atlantic and trans-Pacific routes, later to be taken over by the well-known 747. As the 707s were replaced, some were scrapped whilst others found further use with freight-carrying companies. One such company is Florida West Airlines which, from its base in Miami, operate a fleet of three. Formed in 1981, Florida West fly their 707s to destinations in South and Central America. About to land at the company's home base in December 1990 is an unidentified 707, which no doubt has performed many trips over the Atlantic carrying passengers.

125

Founded in 1965, Connie Kalitta Services operate only freight-carrying flights, originally using a wide variety of aircraft ranging from a Cessna with a maximum take-off weight of 2359kg to a Boeing 747 with a maximum take-off weight of 340,194kg. This North American company with offices in Detroit no longer operate propeller-driven aircraft and the smallest type in use today is the McDonnell Douglas DC-9. In 1991, the company changed its title to become known as American International Airways. Photographed in August 1990, McDonnell Douglas 54 DC-8 series N806CK is parked at Los Angeles International airport awaiting loading of cargo.

Rich International is a Miami, Florida-based charter operator currently using a fleet of three McDonnell Douglas DC-8s and three Lockheed L1011 Tri-Stars. The company was formed in 1971 and originally offered scheduled freight services between Florida and the Caribbean. These were discontinued later when the airline concentrated on providing passenger flights. Services to South America are made by the airline's Tri-Stars, and N313EA, which previously flew for Eastern Airlines, was photographed in December 1991 having just left the company's hanger at Miami airport and making its way to the terminal to operate on the South American service.

One of Rich's DC-8s had completed a flight from a European city as it came into land at the airline's Florida base.

Originally known as Majestic Air, this company, founded in 1988, changed its name to Carnival Airlines in the spring of 1989 and adopted a revised colour scheme. The airline commenced services from its Fort Lauderdale, Florida, base with one Boeing 727 providing daily flights to the Bahamas, later extending services to Miami within their routes. Seven Boeing 727s and seven 737s are now included in Carnival's fleet, all of which are painted in the distinctive red, white and blue livery. One of the airline's 727s, N5609, seen about to depart Ford Lauderdale for the Bahamas in December 1990, was the aircraft first flown by the airline and which carried the Majestic Air colour scheme. This Boeing no longer flies, having been withdrawn in August 1991.

Southwest Airlines originally flew high frequency services within Texas from its base at Love Field, Dallas. Founded in 1967, the airline now provides flights to other North American states using their very large fleet of Boeing 737s which are configured into all economy class seating. Southwest's bright colours can be seen in California, Nevada, Arizona, together with other Western states, and N300SW, one of the airline's series 300 737s, was operating a flight out of Las Vegas when photographed in April 1985.

'AMTRAN' is the callsign of the Indianapolis-based charter airline American Trans Air. Founded in 1973, the company received its certificate in 1981 and currently employs its fleet of Boeing and Lockheed airliners on charters from North America to many worldwide destinations, the majority of which are in Europe. Lockheed Tri-Star N8188AT was operating an American charter when photographed in April 1986, about to commence its start-up run on the runway at Las Vegas airport.

The Eskimo's smiling face, featured on the tails of Alaska Airlines planes, catch the late evening sun as part of the company's fleet park at the gates of Seattle airport in August 1989 whilst awaiting their next duties. The company is based at this Washington state city, providing services within Washington, California, and the 49th state of Alaska.

Continental is one of North America's major airlines and its history can be traced back as far as 1934. The Houston, Texas-based company provides extensive services to Europe and Australia, together with internal flights utilising their all-jet fleet of Boeing, McDonnell Douglas and Airbus Industry aircraft. In 1987, the airline took over Peoplexpress and all their aircraft were integrated into the Continental fleet. Deregulation in North America had an effect on Continental and the company has filed for Chapter 11 Bankruptcy Protection on at least two occasions, whilst operations continued. The last time this occurred was during December 1990 when Continental's planes were carrying their gold, red and orange livery introduced in 1968, and shown here on McDonnell Douglas DC-10 N68065 at Atlanta, Georgia, in June 1987, and again on one of their Boeing 737 series 300s N14307 about to come to a halt after landing at Colorado's mile-high city — Denver, in August 1986.

In an attempt to get out of Chapter 11, the company introduced a new livery in the spring of 1991 hoping that their passengers would see this as a decisive effort to present a new image which would attract new business. Their new livery of grey, gold, blue and white was applied to one of the carrier's Airbus A300s N13983 which is seen on finals to runway 30 at Miami in December 1991.

The Hawaiian Islands, formerly called the Sandwich Islands, were at one time a territory of the United States. Now, the volcanic chain of twenty islands are the 50th state of the USA, the largest island being Hawaii. The capital Honolulu is situated on the island of Oahu and it is here where Hawaiian Air, founded in 1929, is based. Caught between the very heavy Australian autumn showers is Hawaiian Air McDonnell Douglas DC-8 N8973U, a 1969-built series 62 machine. The scene is the international terminal at Sydney in April 1990 where the airliner is being towed to its stand to be prepared for its flight across the Pacific. The aircraft joined the Hawaiian fleet in April 1987 having previously served with United Airlines.

Canada 3000 commenced services in 1988 and was originally known as Air 2000 of Toronto. Its sister company is Air 2000, the Manchester, England-based charter airline, and aircraft of the Canadian subsidiary carry the same basic livery as the United Kingdom airline. Aircraft are leased to each company throughout the year; Canadian Boeing 757s being flown by Air 2000 and vice-versa. The title Air 2000 of Toronto became Air 3000 in May 1989, later to become Canada 3000 as shown on Boeing 757 C-FXOO, about to depart Fort Lauderdale in January 1990. The Canadian airline operate flights to British airports as well as to destinations in America.

Founded in 1984, the Nationair Canada was formed to provide charter flights from its Montreal, Quebec base, with a fleet of extended range Boeing 757s, 747s and McDonnell Douglas DC-8s. All of the company's airliners were configured into economy class seating and flew holidaymakers between Europe and Canada, and from Canada to American destinations. Aircraft were regularly leased in to provide extra capacity during peak periods. Boeing 747 N303TW, photographed in June 1991 was seen arriving at London's Gatwick airport after the completion of a trans-Atlantic flight. The Jumbo had been with Nationair for a year having previously served in the fleet of Trans World Airlines whose basic colours it still carries. The Canadian carrier continued operations until the beginning of 1993 when, owing to substantial debts, its creditors declared the airline bankrupt.

Canadian is one of Canada's major carriers, being formed after the merger in 1987 of Pacific Western Airlines and Canadian Pacific. The period following this merger resulted in many aircraft carrying hybrid liveries which disappeared in the months that followed. The current colours of Canadian are illustrated here on McDonnell Douglas DC-10 C-FCRB preparing to depart Sydney in April 1988.

Founded in 1937 by the Canadian government, Air Canada provides both domestic and international services from its Montreal base with an all-jet fleet of McDonnell Douglas, Boeing, Lockheed and Airbus Industry aircraft. The airline was the first in Canada to take delivery of the Airbus, and put the A320 version into service on the Montreal–Toronto route in February 1990. Around this time, the airline's original titling, showing AIR CANADA in capitals, was replaced with the inscription in upper and lower case characters. The Airbus was also to be later put into service on the Toronto–Miami route, and C-FFWN was being used on the return leg of this service when photographed at Miami in December 1991 about to commence its take-off run.

Opposite
It's New Year's Eve at Miami and a Northwest Boeing 727 has just about made touchdown before sundown.
Well — that's about it, cameras away until next year!